Amazing Athletes ✧ Atletas increíbles

Alex Rodríguez

Baseball Star ✧ Estrella del béisbol

Mary Ann Hoffman

Traducción al español: Eduardo Alamán

PowerKiDS press™ & **Editorial Buenas Letras**™
New York

Published in 2007 by The Rosen Publishing Group, Inc.
29 East 21st Street, New York, NY 10010

Book Design: Daniel Hosek
Layout Design: Lissette González

Photo Credits: Cover, p. 17 © Al Bello/Getty Images; p. 5 © Jonathan Daniel/Allsport; p. 7 © Lisa Blumenfeld/Getty Images; p. 9 © Eliot J. Scheechter/Getty Images; p. 11 © Jed Jacobsohn/Getty Images; pp. 13, 15 © Scott Halleran/Getty Images; p. 19 © Otto Greule Jr./ Getty Images; p. 21 © Scott Gries/Getty Images.

Library of Congress Cataloging-in-Publication Data

Hoffman, Mary Ann, 1947-
  Alex Rodriguez : baseball star / Mary Ann Hoffman; traducción al español:
Eduardo Alamán — 1st ed.
      p. cm. - (Amazing Athletes / Atletas increíbles)
  Includes bibliographical references and index.
  ISBN-13: 978-1-4042-7598-0
  ISBN-10: 1-4042-7598-3
  1. Rodriguez, Alex, 1975-— 2. Baseball players—United States—Biography—Juvenile literature.
    3. Spanish-language materials I. Title. II. Series.

Manufactured in the United States of America

Contents

Contenido

Alex Rodríguez was named MVP of the American League two times. An MVP is the most valuable player.

Alex Rodríguez ha sido elegido dos veces el Jugador más Valioso de la Liga Americana.

Alex is also called A-Rod. He is the youngest player to hit 400 home runs.

A Alex le llaman A-Rod. Alex es el jugador más joven de la historia en batear 400 jonrones.

7

A-Rod was a National Baseball
Student Athlete of the Year
in high school.

En la escuela secundaria, A-Rod
fue el Mejor Atleta de la Liga
Nacional Estudiantil de Béisbol.

8

9

A-Rod played shortstop for the Seattle Mariners in 1994. He was only 18 years old.

En 1994, A-Rod jugó como parador en corto en los Marineros de Seattle. Alex tenía sólo 18 años.

13

A-Rod hit 156 home runs in 3 years for the Rangers. He was the American League MVP in 2003.

A-Rod bateó 156 jonrones en sus 3 años con los Rangers. Alex fue elegido como el Jugador más Valioso de la Liga Americana en 2003.

15

A-Rod was traded to the New York Yankees in 2004. He plays third base for the Yankees.

En 2004, A-Rod llegó a los Yanquis de Nueva York. Alex juega en la tercera base en los Yanquis.

A-Rod hit forty-eight home runs in 2005! He set the American League record.

¡En 2005, A-Rod bateó 48 jonrones! Así, Alex marcó un nuevo récord en la Liga Americana.

A-Rod works with the Boys and Girls Clubs of America. He helps children learn and play sports.

A-Rod trabaja con la organización Boys and Girls Clubs of America. Alex ayuda a que los chicos y chicas aprendan a practicar deportes.

& GIRLS CLUBS

THANK YOU

Alex Rodriguez

BOYS & GIRLS CLUB OF AMERICA

BOYS & GIRLS CLUB OF AMERICA

BOYS & GIRLS CLUB OF AMERICA

Glossary / Glosario

American League (uh-MEHR-uh-kuhn LEEG) A group of baseball teams that regularly play each other.

athlete (ATH-leet) A person trained to play a sport.

home run (HOHM RUHN) A hit in baseball that lets the batter run around all the bases and score a run.

record (REH-kuhrd) The most or best of something.

shortstop (SHORT-stahp) A player who plays between second and third base.

---

atleta (el/la) Una persona que se entrena para practicar un deporte.

jonrón / *home run* (el) Cuando el jugador batea la pelota y corre las cuatro bases para anotar una carrera.

Liga Americana (la) Una organización de equipos de béisbol.

parador en corto / *shortstop* (el) Beisbolista que juega entre la segunda y la tercera base.

récord (el) El mejor resultado o puntuación conseguidos por una persona.

22

Resources / Recursos

BOOKS IN ENGLISH / LIBROS EN INGLÉS

Armentrout, David, and Patricia Armentrout. *Alex Rodriguez.* Vero Beach, FL: Rourke Publishing, LLC, 2004.

Kjelle, Marylou Morano. *Alex Rodriguez.* Hockessin, DE: Mitchell Lane Publishers, Inc., 2006.

BOOKS IN SPANISH / LIBROS EN ESPAÑOL

Christopher, Matt. *En el campo de juego con... Alex Rodríguez.* Little, Brown Young Readers, 2005

Suen, Anastasia. *La historia del béisbol.* New York: Rosen Publishing/Editorial Buenas Letras, 2004.

Index

Índice

11/14 (8) 10/14
3/19 (N) 6/17